Beauty Still Lives Here

Beauty Still Lives Here

Poems by

Kelsi Folsom

© 2025 Kelsi Folsom. All rights reserved.
This material may not be reproduced in any form, published,
reprinted, recorded, performed, broadcast,
rewritten, or redistributed without
the explicit permission of Kelsi Folsom.
All such actions are strictly prohibited by law.

Cover design by Shay Culligan
Cover image by Cody F. Miller
www.codyfmiller.com
Author photo by Wesley F. Folsom

ISBN: 978-1-63980-717-8

Kelsay Books
502 South 1040 East, A-119
American Fork, Utah 84003
Kelsaybooks.com

To Avelissa, Josiah, Arthur, and Daniel—my living poems

To Callie, Mark, Ashley, Katy, and Erin—fellow writers and collaborative encouragers in the trenches of telling

To Wesley—my partner in the refining fire

Acknowledgments

It is with a heart full of gratitude that I name the original homes these poems found and thank the gracious editors who carefully selected them:

Anabaptist World: "Vessels"
Catchwater Magazine: "Home," "Mother at the Radio"
The Clayjar Review: "Where Love Lives," "The Crushing"
Coffee and Crumbs: "Commitment"
Ekstasis: "Devotion"
Heart of Flesh Literary Magazine: "Swingsets"
The Keeping Room: "At Best Farm in Monocacy, Maryland"
Momma Theologians: "Mother in a Rocking Chair," "Communion"
Motherscope: "Maternity Panties"
The Orchards Poetry Journal: "Little Owl"
Snapdragon: A Journal of Art and Healing: "Tectonic Plates," "Finally"
Solid Food Press: "God of the Cupboards," "Bearing Witness"
Wild Roof Journal: "Prehistoric"

Contents

I

Loose Feathers	17
Poems	18
Home	19
What Makes the House Ours	20
The Catch	22
Plans	23
Lanapo Sandals	24
The Magazine	25
On Convenience	26
Nostalgia at Chik-fil-A	27
The Menu	28
Hunger, a Still Life	29
Unfinished/French Toast	30
God of the Cupboards	31
Mother at the Radio	33
Spilling	34
Dishes	35
Devotion	36
Communion	38
Bearing Witness	40

II

Mother at a Picnic Table	43
On Keeping America Great	45
Mother Washing Her Face	46
On the Death of a Writer	47
Surrender	48
The Couch Where Sickness Lives	49
Mother by the Nightstand	50

In the Marrow of Midnight	51
The Distance Between Here and There: a Triptych	52
Burnout	57
Tectonic Plates	58
Trying on Contrition	59
Swingsets	60
Commitment	63

III

Prehistoric	67
At Best Farm in Monocacy, Maryland	69
Autumn at Cabin John Park	70
The Scent of June	71
Afterglow, the Sacrament	72
Where Love Lives	73
Saturday Morning	74
Little Owl	75
Of the Expectant	76
Maternity Lingerie	77

IV

January Matins	81
Winter Meditation	82
Vessels	83
Snowy Afternoon	84
Lemon Raspberry Cake	85
Encore	86
This Spirit	87
Mother in a Rocking Chair	89

The Sounds of Now	90
Restoration	91
Finally	92
Provision	93
The Crushing	94

*At this hour what is dead is restless
and what is living is burning*

—Li Young Lee, "This Hour and What Is Dead"

I

Loose Feathers

The birds speak
a language I don't know.

I strain to understand
their chittering tongues,

the reasons why this song
and that leaf are the right fit,

why these twigs and
those branches are home?

How loose feathers
and long love worm

their way into
screeching beaks,

how stillness can fly
at the right speed?

Poems

They came for the berries,
        the birds did
Through the windows I see them
Tv screen blaring *Parenthood*
because I'm too tired to clean.
My excuse for every inadequacy—
        I need more sleep
        More food
        More money
        More mornings off

It's been weeks since I've written a poem.

I've been reading a lot of Catherine de Vinck
trying to write more like her
        be more like her—
profound in a prophetic sense,
not just spitting nice lines in surprising ways
but blasting the soul with unexpected grace
where an angle yet considered changes everything.

Home

The only way to love a mystery
is to free it from being solved.

Find a city with a good heartbeat
then step on its neck—

If it screams back at you,
You've found your home.

scratch that

Find the heartbeat of a city
and put down roots in the center

of the only place you can breathe—

build a house
brick by brick
into a solid sac of lungs.

Pick anywhere you want to go
and pin it on the map,

Google will tell you
how to get there.

What Makes the House Ours

We took down paintings from the wall
like a woman takes off her makeup,

the party's over 'till
the next one starts.

What we hang on the walls
is what makes the house ours—

this memento from Maui
that quote that keeps me going

the to-do list on the fridge
and the candles on the mantle—

Very slowly the house
returns to its vacant state.

We examine the blank walls like
a woman peers into the mirror and sees

the work of staying strong,
how the years add up

in serums
and a set jaw,

saved tears for another day
stuffing the cupboards

past expiration dates,
all the things we meant

to throw away but
just ran out of time.

We slough off the excess
return return return

clear the table
make some space
for the new dreams simmering,
hovered over the gas flame

the party's over 'till
the next one starts.

The Catch

Like a hook lodged in the cheek of a bluegill
is my desire to live where I've been.

I'm supposed to get a new license plate
consent to the identifier of a new state

but this hook tugs me back to the boat
I've known for the past few years.

I know the hands on the other end of the line,
I trust the way they crank the reel

the knowledge of their fingers
dragging along my spine

considering the weight
of my flesh and scales.

Plans

Timing,
it's all about
the timing.

Everything comes
down to timing—
love, sex, food,
art, breakthrough,
travel, death.

We don't know
when . . .

I hate making plans
yet I depend on them
to buoy these days
that might pull me under,

a plan
        (there's an idea)
a plan
        (if the timing's right)

a plan pins down
stars to our flesh,
like an effervescent
map of "maybes."

Lanapo Sandals

Looped around my heel is
a thin slip of leather dyed
and cut and sewn into a shoe
at a seaside village in Italy.

Stripes, like panini
        irons slice my
                foot into thirds.

Aubergine lines mesmerize
flirtatious hems flutter
softly near my thighs
giving voice to inward sighs
about the lies I spend
the days telling my children.

Like all shall be well,
and it will be alright,
while they search
my eyes for comfort
and my heart
for stars in the night.

The Magazine

Are we all just victims of marketing,
had the designs pulled
over our eyes?

It's all waiting for a touch,
a calloused finger
to glide upon the edge
and peek inside
ink stamped pages
of brilliant commercials,

bright smiling photos of
unabashed consumerism—
none of it matters
without the curious reader,
eager patrons of mundane magic.

On Convenience

Nothing but Amazon fits the bill,
at will all our fancies fly
straight to our doors.

But more often than not,
what's most worth
our time wanes hungrily

on the back burner
wishing we'd grab a ladle and
a pinch of salt from time to time.

Nostalgia at Chik-fil-A

I just caught a whiff of Christmas
with a side of waffle fries
while I stand in line to order
like my mama years before
holding little hands
and pennies at the
bottom of her purse
hoping dinner might be
found between her fingers.

The Menu

Each time I scrape
a small dish of dinner
into the trash,
I imagine the beggar
fishing for food,
mouth open,
eyes wide,
pulling beans and apples
and cheese out
as if appearing
in the dump by magic.

Hunger, a Still Life

Two white muffins
and a black plastic
bag lie face up
to the rain like
a prophet's lament

fully exposed
they point to the sky
soggy wrappers clinging
to cold dusty cries.

This morning
perhaps they
were meant to
be breakfast

of blueberry and milk
eggs and flour
baked into mounds
jittery hands could devour

but now
not even the birds
give them a passing glance,
these humble dreams
hardening by the highway.

Unfinished/French Toast

The bag of bread rings
like an unexpected rainstorm
when I pull it from the
wooden drawer to open
it for lunch.

The tie untwists
crumbs fall out
honey wheat slices
release a wave of welcome
with their tender corners
begging for a bite.

What shall I slather
their sides with today?
Butter and jam?
Cold cheese and ham?
Shall I drown them in custard
sear them in turn
Finish them off
with a steady drip
of maple syrup
siphoned from a tree?

God of the Cupboards

It's the big can of black beans
on the shelf by the stove whose
lid evades my attempts at prying,

the lid just won't give.

I put the pans away already,
they're loud and cumbersome,
Heavier than I think, fooled
by the strength in my arms
and my hands I carry
too much to the sink,
I carry too much noise to
breakfast and midnight
so I stop at the sink take
a breather at midday.

I sit before
God's eyes
astonished
they still
look for me.

Have I not wasted
enough time
wallowing in pits
of unworthiness?

I got stuck again this morning,
like five minutes before
I need to leave
like always

the list of
"Let me do that
real quick"
keeps multiplying

calcifying all my
senses of freedom.
But what makes me
free isn't productivity—

Like I can't fold
my name into a
sweet potato muffin
and bake it into a

life I can bite—
Holy, holy, holy,
is the cry of my eyes
searching desperately

for God in all the cupboards.

Mother at the Radio

for the wives of Kennedy's Space Race

How do you measure
the minutes of sorrow
or the agony of love
in increments of seconds?

Moment by moment,
it all comes to pass.

The braun of world politics
sitting on his shoulders
while your shoulders
bear the weight riding

static-stuttered airwaves.

I see you.

It's impossible, this mission
littering history with widows,

your cigarette tells you everything
you wish you didn't know:

anxiety.
heat.

Desire for a kind of security
you know
you will never meet.

Spilling

Was it worth it?
The years you
gave and gave and gave?
Can you cash in on
your heroic efforts
to make it all okay?

Can all the quarters
flying on the wings
of wishes make
an impact at the
bottom of a fountain?

Dishes

What do you know,
Mr. Spud Brush,
can you tell me why
the world is on fire?
Why women and children
are raped in the crosshairs
of conflict, sticky webs
of evil's ire?
What do you know,
blue liquid of Dawn,
can you whisper
through sudsy bubbles,
why young people drown
under cycles of poverty?
Why grown men cry
and old women give up
hoping anything could
ever be different?
What do you know,
sustainable boar's hair bristles,
can you wash away
the tides of cruelty
swallowing families whole?
What about you,
yellow latex gloves,
can you protect me
from the fear that's
harder to cut than grease?
Mortality lingers long after
the lathering of a good life,
swirling down the sink draining
dirt by the seconds while
I finish cleaning all
that I've made dirty.

Devotion

*Sometimes the wind scatters light across the lake's wrinkles,
tosses clarity to Peter's loss of Christ.*
—Isabel Chenot, "Lake Michigan"

I can't make the distance
work for me.

It's too long.

It's too far.

I can't see what's around
the bend, all the bends
never end. I take a knee

dizzy under the weight
of amends I can't
make work for me.

Piety promised peace
but what it gave
me was anxiety
by the stemfuls
of wine promising
peace would come
with one more drink.

> *Give me this tourniquet,*
> *the one I have made*
> *the one with holes in it*
> *the one with no name.*

Because the only one
whose name in pieces
like a matzah snowflake
of absolution and mercy

mirrors wholeness where
cracks crawl through
wounded faces is

the man whose ghost treads
the waves of Galilee

in a salt-baptized
wind blowing
Grace upon grace
upon grace upon
grace becoming
thumbs of ash-smeared

Relief closing
the distance
and working
for me.

Communion

It's a wonder how
we pick and choose
which ways we want
to be broken.

We say we give
our all, that we
love sacrificially
and yet we're eager
to build walls
around the marrow
of our motives.

We ask God to open
the eyes of our hearts
to bless our hands to
do the work
of breaking the bread
and sharing the parts
of the body and the blood
we'd rather keep to ourselves.

We don't want to see,
we want permission
for our ignorance.

The truth is too apparent
in another human's eyes,
it's too hard to swallow
conflicts we cannot fix.

But maybe if we set tables
instead of building fences,
Maybe if we clasped hands
instead of mounting offensives,
We'd find more beneath our hands
than lines in the sand, find

the borders of our flesh
aren't in need of more saviors
rather
threads of kinship
stitched and sticking
like a coat of many colors.

Bearing Witness

Bearing witness is a weighted glory
Deep calling low breath stillness at the edge.

What will happen next?

What words will spill over creation
to make a song of breathing?

Like the middle of a fine blend
of flour salt and sugar where
a well scooped out is prepared

to host an egg and a seed,
milk and melted butter

The fat, wheft, and give of a real bite
The reason why a slice of it costs you
$7.99 or more . . . it's the hope growing

filling your mouth with good things
rich, creamy things that settle in for
the long process of being divined.

That song will cost you,
but look at the life it makes.

II

Mother at a Picnic Table

She wakes up with rosy dreams
of perfect parenting where she knows
exactly what to do
and exactly where to go

but,

more often than not she's
the lady rolling up to the park
with screaming kids smacking
her face while she unbuckles their belts.

(is she really that terrible?)

She watches frustration
fracturing the faces
of her littles and thinks,
"me too, ya'll, me too."

Can she skip today,
take a mental health leave?
She doesn't want to be bothered,
she doesn't want to meet a need.

She's going on a business trip
feeling guilty guilty guilty
thinking maybe she shouldn't leave,
but she's so desperate for the quiet . . .

and don't empowered women make their own decisions?

She's stretched
like a wet hide
across intellectual
divides so she'll

strike her drum
on the isolated ground of
everyone's a little bit right.

On Keeping America Great

Bow your head and pray,
reach a hand across your limits
and say "come, have a meal at my table,"
then pour a glass of red wine
and receive whatever pain may
fall across your lap.

Mother Washing Her Face

She doesn't feel beautiful,
she feels ship-shod.

The paint is peeling,
the wood is rotting

the seagulls have settled
into the Captain's Quarters

and she doesn't have the energy
to smooth out the borders.

Somedays she yearns
to live forever, burns

with the desire
to wield holy fire

liar

most days she's
jealous of the dying—

They get to dry their
hands much sooner.

On the Death of a Writer

for Rachel Held Evans

I'm the lady who lost her
cool maniacally at Whole Foods
near the register grieving
a friend she doesn't even know.

I don't know, I didn't know her,
but
somehow she knew me, you see?

So there's snot on the steering wheel,
that's what I'm saying,
frozen peas growing warm
in the passenger's seat
waiting.
       Waiting, waiting, waiting,
for the driver to reach into the glovebox,
grab a napkin and carry on.

Surrender

When she died he   reached across the
   chasm of sunglasses   and empty cups
      to meet my palm   and hold my tears,
         our ages meeting in the
            middle.

The Couch Where Sickness Lives

for Tim Pedersen

I know now what it feels like
to dig a cemetery right in my heart,
to palm clods of dirt for the
inevitable bed of a friend
who's barely talking,

To line the couch where sickness
lives with petitions and remembrances
split cheeks of laughter
truths standing blue amidst
confessions and tear-smudged maybes

sparrows of life
arranged in a line
of gaping disbelief—

    you're dying

To witness light
rivening down
the body of this man
as his brittle bones
are cradled close
love lit between his
eyes brightened by
the unquenchable flame
of knowing
he's going home.

Mother by the Nightstand

A muted white rectangle
holds the light in,
pulls loneliness to gaze
at what would have been bright.

Perfume and potions,
stacks of half-read books,
gummed up tubes
of concealer and mascara
sit quietly nearby,

Slippers she meant to give away,
rubber sandals splitting at the tongue,
an aching in her lower back
nudging her to lie down

but

She wants to stay up,
keep writing and dreaming,
it's less lonely that way
keep writing and dreaming keep

writing and dreaming . . .

In the Marrow of Midnight

      the clench of my bones
            meets the sawhorse of memory
                  doing its quiet work alone.

                My thoughts clotting cream
         clinging cold to the
   back of a spoon
come and get me
come and get me
she cries to the moon.

The Distance Between Here and There: a Triptych

I.

The silent bloom
of percolating coffee
lets me know my feet
should be on the floor.
The crack of dawn has peaked
while wood creaks silently
under the stride of my husband
opening the door.

He loves me so well
medium-dark roast
in the cauldron
of a Chemex, gently poured
into a porcelain mug painted
with a bird of paradise.

The door closes with
a kiss upon my forehead—
The kids will be up soon.

Remnants of dreams linger
heavily around the steam
as I fumble for the spectacles
on my nightstand.
The lamp turns on,
a white leather journal looks at me
each page naked before my thoughts—

Will I write about it today?

I hear the giggles of my children
as their father gets them dressed
their adoration is evident.

I can hardly stand it.

II.

On a Sunday in June,
a dark green Subaru
fires its engines
and roars down
the driveway carrying
a pair of lungs
I've come to depend on.

Away they inhale
and exhale for 15 hours
towards a medical rotation
in Atlanta, Georgia.

We kiss
and I see a tiny apartment
at the foot of Paris Hill
on a little island named Saba
nestled in the heart
of the Dutch Caribbean.

An angel stood
over the doorway saying
"all will be well."
I cried, leaning
against the stove knowing
I would not be the engine
of its warmth—keeping the lights on
          buttering the sandwiches
          making the bed.

He would come and go,
and I would not know.

It all spread out between our eyes:
images, feelings, fleeting storms,
the colors and smells of
heart-pounding despair,
the exhilarating romance
of the "us" we've been building.

I wave and head back
to finish my coffee
before it turns cold.
I tiptoe back into our bed
curbing my loneliness
in the white of our sheets.

I look at the bookshelf
where six years ago,
newly engaged, the shelves
were lined with pictures
and love letters, daily statements
of our long-distance love.

I pull the blankets tighter
around my heart, un-interrupted
by advances for romance.
The deep slumber of loneliness
rests atop my breasts

I can hardly stand it.

III.

I wake up early to make the coffee,
scoop by scoop,
grounds drowned by boiling water,
a feat of aggravation and heat.
This moment of holiness
is punctuated by cries for
"mommy," and "come sit by me,"
also, "I'm hungry" while
I'm scrambling the eggs
like I'm oblivious to the basic care
and keeping of little ones.

These long, hot days stretch
out around trips to the splash pad,
the food markets, and
meal-prepping for sanity's sake . . .

The strands around my face
refuse to mind themselves today.

Off to the fridge to forage for apple juice,
leftovers asking me what's for dinner.
I pour three cups
set them near the eggs
bring my children near to eat.

They smile, saying "thank you, mommy,"
at least, they meant to.
They ask for Daddy
and chuck a fork in my direction.

Burnout

Today
no amount
of vice can
soothe my pain—
not glasses of wine,
not foul language, not
moist chocolate cake,
not emails from friends,
not making a sale,
not booking an event,
not scrolling through
Instagram, not white
fuzzy robes, not
sweet chubby cheeks,
not a novel with
my feet up . . .

Murder,
I suppose,
will suffice
for this week

A dull pocketknife
mincing nice-ness
with bigness.

Tectonic Plates

the couch creaks
under the weight
of our differences.
He vents
I breathe
and clutch
the leg of God.

My turn.

Tensions rise,
my voice gets big.
Liabilities scooch closer
thumbs extended for a war
as the skeletons
to the left of us
smile and take notes
as our very valid points
are bandied back and forth.

Trying on Contrition

I. We always
    fight in parks.
    I think it's the
    mirage of peace
    that drives us quietly
    into madness.

II. I said I'm sorry,
    but I didn't mean it.

    What I mean is,
    don't let it ruin your day.

Swingsets

Maybe it's the rhythm
the predictable back and forth
whoosh and *thwack* as the
seat catches in my hand
that comforts the stability
I don't have at home.

Maybe that's not true
or maybe just unfair
but my hand knows
with my eyes closed
exactly when my son
will swing back and
Pause
       half a second held
in the breadth of my
ready spread palm,

No magnet but the pull
of timing and intimacy
even trust because
I have not left where I stand.

And if I stay long enough
the work will change its mind
and become rest, change
its mind and become belonging
to this moment

quiet

honest

prayer.

Nature's Lyre

I know why King David
heard the trees clap their hands—
the ache in his soul needed
a standing ovation.

Commitment

Maybe "I love you,"
isn't enough

But

Maybe "I'm with you,"
is.

III

Prehistoric

Is the earth
just like a
big spinning brain,
teetering on the edge
of panic and peace?

If I pull a bone
from the ground
would I steal
from another time
running around mine
in concentric circles?

Maybe thousands
of years ago
an Allosaurus stumbles
as a thigh bone
is removed,
Meticulously
lying down
To a studious
future of extinction.

I am amazed by time,
by eternity's tactile
web of connections.

Nothing is fixed,
but the spin
of persistence—
angling,
Arching,
hovering,
Yearning,
touching,
Longing,

all for the sake of knowing
it was.

But the miracle
of time is
Relevance
and
Remembering
like finding
the hidden meaning
Under layers and layers of dirt.

At Best Farm in Monocacy, Maryland

I. Beautiful day for war,
fields of yellowing leaves
speckled with black spots
buffering centuries of secrets
stuck in the soil
whispering to any root
that'll listen to its' stories

*Put down your weapons,
pick up your ploughs.*

II. The earth has never faltered
under kind cultivation,
making angry footsteps soft
in the mercy of her ground.

She sets a table daily
in the crack of ancient pavement
Flowers blooming
feasting
celebrating
"beauty still lives here."

Autumn at Cabin John Park

I. Bark shooting towards the sky
       then changing its mind
       veering towards a yellow
       cupola of preschool delight.

II. That moment before a fear takes flight—
       head first, arms back
       blessed by the gentle fall
       of a life coming full circle.

III. Each take their turn sliding down
       into a bed of giggles, reaching
       out and squealing, "Come with me!"
       an irresistible invitation.

The Scent of June

Roses bloom in a moment
far behind the touch of memory

Delicate and sensuous,
sweaty and expectant,

the roses tell of an anxious queen
coming to meet her lover at midday.

Armored with nothing but
lace and desire,

she steps timidly across
a history of limestone.

Eyes at once brilliant and broken
meet her own

hands that hold
sweet ships in their harbor

Reach out and out
and over and over,

Not once on this day,
but minutes ever after

the dust of "I do"
settles on the altar.

Afterglow, the Sacrament

We lay together like sheaves
exhausted by perfection
perfected by exhaustion
joining flesh with spirit
peeling back the theories
of our origin.

Imagined, then fashioned
note by note into skin
set in motion by a song of beauty
filling up our souls like

love's answer to the furious cry
of emptiness and wanting,
fruitful words become a well
of bursting life from arid ground.

I would die in your arms,
the cradle of civilization,
the humming bones
of the unknown nestled
hip to hip in peaceful consultation.

Where Love Lives

My soul thirsts for God, for the living God.
When can I go and meet with God?
                            —Psalm 42:2

In about five minutes
my eyes will be closed,
my cheek will be pressed
against the white cotton
comforter yielding to sleep,
that bone-weary medicine
bringing the truth into focus,
that gentle shepherd
of nighttime contours
lighting my way
and inhabiting a dream,
that midnight moon glow
bringing the blanket
near my chin
where love lives
between my face
and the pillowcase.

Saturday Morning

Stubble like a paintbrush
sweeps across his jaw,

sheets like many waters
spread a healing from his hips,

hair like downy feathers
nestles sweetly near his lips,

our babies
warm and costly

settle softly on his chest.

He holds them close,
each one a pearl

carefully cultured in
the hollow of his neck,

his gift of presence
his curious face—

The wonder of a father meeting
what love can cultivate.

Little Owl

hoo hoo
the little owl calls
when the morning pulls
the covers down
and breaks out in a grin.

Formed like a flute
around tongue and tone,
the song of mother eve
creates once more.

Little owl
with furrowed brow
translates the song of
penguin and brown bear

shimmering zinnias
warm pumpkin waffles
Towering pines
ravenous cardinals

squeaking floorboards
crashing race cars
scurrying squirrels
tumbling giggles

The silky sacrament
of life's long tail
caught in the teeth
of a baby.

Of the Expectant

Life grows
in mysterious ways,
building and
nurturing
the foundations
of humanity.

Sinew stretches
skin pulls tight,
organs realign
as newborn iterations
expand.

In the womb,
the shade of
tomorrow
is formed.

Maternity Lingerie

What do I do with these?
The elastic is shedding
like kraft string cheese
sagging wiggles of spandex
and loose cotton dreams.

The black and tan ones
gave me all sorts of
lines and maybes
like the touch of lace
was actually very sexy,

and I was smart to
find underwear that
barely rose over my
pubic bone, the fruit of
my womb could hang

over and over
heavy and prolific
as much
as much
as much

as it liked.

IV

January Matins

Snow floats past the windows
like icy down on broken ground,

the whole day baptized
in frosty white perfection

shaking out the dust
from yesterday's toils

fragrant

        fresh

                quiet.

Winter Meditation

Teach me of your
Presence in the wet
bite of the wind.

How faith in you looks
like staying warm
keeping watch over
tiny forms wrapped in blankets.

Grant me the grace
of a woolen sock when
I can't feel my feet.

Pull gratitude up from
the coals of my need
in the grey snark of the dawn.

Vessels

Creation crunches beneath my toes
cool and ripe and grainy mash of
nuts, scat, feathers, and pinecones
sifting curiosity from winter's bone
in the soft breath of the wind.

These sermons in the soil,
exhortations of clay and worms,
recipes of grace from the muddy
hands of the sun suddenly preaching:

Gather your heart
      with the crumbs
           from breakfast
                Gather your soul
      with the secrets
  of sparrows

Gather your mind
      with the stems
          of roses
                Come clean in
        the whispers
  of snowfall.

Snowy Afternoon

I love the way the
word December looks,
the way it sounds
like an exotic spice:
Just a pinch of December
to dust atop the crust
before baking in the oven
for 30 minutes or until a
toothpick in the center
comes out clean.

Lemon Raspberry Cake

I plunge my fork into the moist silk dragging
the bottom of the silver tines languidly across my tongue

softly sucking the flirtation of the glaze like an eager
lover fumbling with her lips

coaxing the crumbs and
slow-pour together,

quenching,
savoring each sip

What is it about the taste of lemon
that pairs so well with hot coffee?

The tension of the wet steam mingling
with the cool tang of tart surrendering to sweet.

At last all is right with the morning
and the world,

a small joy inhabited
my mouth open wide.

Encore

Why does every precious
thing want to leave so quickly?

My cup of coffee has
reached its end and still

I want more.

This Spirit

And learn power, however sweet they call you, learn power,
the smash of the holy once more, and signed by its name.
—Annie Dillard, from "Holy the Firm"

The clouds accumulate for a quick kiss
of candy and cream-colored paint.

They hover over Lake Erie
like an egg waiting to be cracked.

Not a hurry
                      in sight

I sit in a white plastic chair,
right leg hung over my left thigh.

Life is feeling
                      lived
one line at a time
                      but

I want the whole narrative arc in one sitting.

This spirit wants to cause a ruckus
raise a glass to the sky and smash it.

This spirit wants to storm the stage
snap a bowstring in a furious *fortississimo*.

Some days this same spirit wants to pen a defense
of the humble way the sand relieves the shoreline.

But mostly
                        this spirit
wants to die out
                slowly

like a
            good song sounding
                              on the tide.

Mother in a Rocking Chair

Her hand is gripped
like a lifeboat of solace,
woven with innocence
and tiny bone perfection,
a road-weary rudder
for empty tummies
and fitful sleeping.

Her hand extends—*hush, hush,*
Fear suspends—*sleep,sleep.*

Is this how Jesus felt when
the three words winds responded to
were "Peace, be still"
and the ocean's rage was held
within his wholeness?

yes

That's how she feels
when the wailing stops,
her body's son relaxing
in the hum of her voice
hovering over the waters.

The Sounds of Now

White noise

a helicopter

the intermittent rustling of a newborn

the clink of a fork against a breakfast plate

the rumble of a city getting out of bed.

Sometimes a swig of coffee

reminds me of traveling,

the simplicity of a literal

destination, the monotonous whir

of little kingdoms passing under

the wheels, the excitement

of being in between.

Restoration

        If your name
        gets lost in the
        clamor of
        globalization,
Stretch your back
against earth's body,
and drink deep
of terrestrial grace.

Finally

I can taste it,
the fruit,
rolling off the boughs
of prayer-bent hands
turning ploughs
of the seconds
into sacred seed beds.

Dreams.

yes

Possibilities.

yes

Provision

  The Costco-size jar   of strawberry jam
      lasts exactly six   weeks to the day,
         like it knows   just how much
               to preserve to be perfectly
                    rationed.

The Crushing

I squeezed the orange
mash between my fingers
working out my grief in
mini strokes of the
thumb and forefinger,
retribution fat in
each fist making
a long game out
of power
                and

                              submission.

I hate it—
the power.

We were never made
for such stature
as to crush.

Mary,
            you know
                        the virgin,
was tasked with crushing
the serpent's head—
Something to celebrate
but what woman doesn't
Find this work exhausting?
the drawn out turmoil of
timing
            and
                        authority

enmeshed in some sour
soup of righteousness
and impossibility.

I am
but one woman
tasked with the
Crushing, the
Audacity to notice
the slithering evils
and think redemption
could be
          (is)
                          Between my toes.

Psalm 46 says God
is my refuge
and my strength,
that the earth
"melts" under His voice.
That's smooth as butter
if I ever heard, and
butter beats nice with
Brown sugar now

we're talking
          possibilities
                     here,
something that makes
Food when subjected
to heat, something
That makes a table
of love when
          burned
                        at the right temperature.

About the Author

Kelsi Folsom is a Texas-born poet and classically-trained singer navigating marriage and motherhood with black coffee, her library card, and a whole lot of prayer.

Her poems and essays are published in *The Orchards Poetry Journal, Plough, West Texas Literary Review, Verily Magazine, Heart of Flesh Literary Magazine,* and elsewhere. She is the author of three collections of poetry, *Breaking the Jar* (Finishing Line Press, 2022), *Buried in the Margins* (Finishing Line Press, 2020), and *Words the Dirt Meant to Share* (Desert Willow Press, 2018).

She is a M.A. student in Theopoetics and Writing at Bethany Theological Seminary. Her work has been featured in numerous anthologies, including *Songs of Love and Strength* (Mum Poem Press), *I Will Set a Place for You* (Solid Food Press), and *I Tried Not to Write* (Snapdragon Journal of Art and Healing).

As an opera and jazz singer, she has performed all over the world, including Scandinavia, Maui, Israel, the Dutch Caribbean, Central America, and Portugal. Most recently, she performed in Verdi's *Requiem* with the Carmel Symphony Orchestra and traveled to Cape Town, South Africa as the lead singer with Global Missions Project's Metro Big Band Jazz Orchestra.

As a minister of Christ Jesus, she strives to utilize the power of creative arts to positively shape culture as a form of hospitality, advocacy, and recovery. She enjoys encouraging others to live embodied lives of purpose, imagination, and delight.

When she isn't making food for family and friends, she enjoys hiking, getting lost in art museums, studying herbalism, and planning vacations poets can't afford. She currently makes her home in NW Ohio with her EM physician husband and four fantastic kiddos.

Instagram: @kelsifolsom
Website: www.kelsifolsom.com
Newsletter: The Shameless Beauty Digest

Made in the USA
Columbia, SC
10 March 2025